Won't You Let Him In?

JAMES W. MOORE

Won't You Let Him In?

AN ADVENT STUDY FOR ADULTS

ABINGDON PRESS / Nashville

WON'T YOU LET HIM IN?
AN ADVENT STUDY FOR ADULTS

Copyright © 2002 by Abingdon Press

This book is printed on acid-free paper.

Library of Congress Cataloging-in-Publication Data

Moore, James W. (James Wendell), 1938–
Won't you let Him in? : an Advent study for adults / James W. Moore.
    p. cm.
ISBN 0-687-05294-7 (alk. paper)
1. Advent.   I. Title.

BV40.M65 2002
242'.332—dc21   2002020658

Scripture quotations, unless otherwise noted, are from the New Revised Standard Version of the Bible, copyright © 1989 by the Division of Christian Education of the National Council of the Churches of Christ in the United States of America, and are used by permission. All rights reserved.

The Scripture quotation noted NIV is taken from the Holy Bible: New International Version®. Copyright © 1973, 1978, 1984 by the International Bible Society. Used by permission of Zondervan Publishing House. All rights reserved.

The Scripture quotation noted NKJV is from the New King James Version. Copyright © 1979, 1980, 1982, Thomas Nelson Inc., Publishers.

Thanks to Lee McKinzie for providing some of the study/discussion questions.

Fourth week of Advent adapted from *Christmas Gifts That Always Fit* by James W. Moore © 1996 by Abingdon Press. Used by permission.

02 03 04 05 06 07 08 09 10 11—10 9 8 7 6 5 4 3 2 1
MANUFACTURED IN THE UNITED STATES OF AMERICA

For June

Contents

Introduction

"For God so loved the world that he gave his only Son . . ." (John 3:16).

The gift of the Christ Child; this is what Christmas is really all about: God's greatest gift to the world, God's most amazing gift to you and me. But it becomes our responsibility

to receive the gift
to welcome the gift
to accept the gift
to celebrate the gift

I heard once about a young man who wanted his parents to give him a car for his birthday. When they presented him with his birthday gift, he could see through the thin, white wrapping paper that the gift was a Bible.

He became angry. He threw down the gift, screamed horrible insults at his parents, vowed never to speak to them again, and ran out of the house and out of their lives. The young man's parents tried to contact him, but he was so angry and bitter that he would not receive their calls or open their letters.

Ten years later, both of his parents were killed in a tragic automobile accident. After the funeral, the young man was going through the possessions in their home; and he found that Bible. It was still wrapped in the delicate white paper. It had never been opened.

He removed the wrapping paper and found a letter addressed to him just inside the front cover of the Bible. He opened the letter, and something fluttered out and fell to the floor. He reached down and picked it up. It was a check. It was dated his birthday, ten years before. The amount of the check was $40,000.00. The letter read:

Dear Brad,

Happy Birthday! We are so proud of you, we wanted to give you two gifts. First, this Bible, which is one of the treasured heirlooms of our family. It belonged to your great-grandmother, who used it to teach Sunday school for many years. We thought you would like to have it. And second, here is a check so you can buy the car of your choice. We love you. Happy Birthday and many Happy Returns.
Love,
Mom and Dad

Isn't that sad? Ten years of separation, ten years of heartache, ten years of alienation, ten years of estrangement—all because he refused to open the gift.

God offers us the gift of Jesus Christ:

> a gift that money can't buy
> a gift that always fits
> a gift wrapped in heaven

Won't you receive the gift?
Won't you accept the gift?
Won't you welcome the gift?
Won't you let him in?

Won't You Let Him In to Your Heart?

Scripture: Read Luke 2:1-7.

The Taj Mahal is one of the most beautiful and costly tombs in the world. The colorful legends that surround the building of the Taj Mahal are all fascinating. But there is one that haunts and disturbs. Shah Jahan, the powerful Mogul emperor of India in the seventeenth century, was in grief. His wife had died. He loved her deeply, and he was devastated by her loss. He decided to honor her in an outstanding way. He would construct an incredible temple, the likes of which the world had never seen. The temple would serve as her tomb; and it would be a memorial tribute to her, as well as a dramatic symbol of his love for her.

The wife's "coffin was placed in the center of a large parcel of land, and construction of the temple began around it. No expense would be spared." The Shah wanted to make her final resting place magnificent and breathtaking. "But as the weeks turned into months, the Shah's grief was eclipsed by his passion for the [building] project." He no longer missed his wife. He hardly thought of her at all anymore. "He no longer mourned her absence." He was now totally consumed with the details of the building project. He was completely obsessed with the construction of the temple. It was all he thought about. It was on his mind night and day, the building of this magnificent temple.

Then one day, while hurriedly walking from one side of the construction site to the other, the Shah accidentally bumped his leg against a wooden box. He was irritated. Impatiently, he "brushed the dust off his leg and ordered the worker[s] to throw the box out." What was that box doing here in the middle of the building, anyway? Get it out of here right now!

Shah Jahan did not realize that the box held the remains of his beloved wife. He threw out her coffin. He forgot she was there.[1]

The one the temple was built for was cast out. The one who inspired the whole project in the first place was now forgotten. The one the temple was intended to honor was harshly pushed aside, absentmindedly thrown away, blatantly ignored—but the temple was erected anyway. Isn't that amazing?

Could someone build a temple and forget why? Could someone sculpt a tribute and forget the hero? Could someone celebrate an anniversary and forget the guest of honor? Could someone create a memorial and forget who is supposed to be remembered?

This dramatic ancient legend is a painfully relevant parable for the way some people celebrate Christmas today; and the point is clear: Sometimes we get so involved in the tasks and details of Christmas that we forget the One we are honoring.

Five little words in the Gospel of Luke say it all: "No room in the inn" (Luke 2:7, NIV; adapted).

There is a certain pathos in those words: "No room for you here." That was the beginning of the Master's life. That was the very first thing the world said to Jesus Christ. That experience would plague him the remainder of his days on this earth and, indeed, even to this present moment. *No room!* "We're just too crowded! Sorry, we're full up. No vacancy. Try again some other time. No room for you here. So, if you'll please excuse me, I've got a million and one things to see about! It's too bad, but there's just no room!"

Sadly, like Shah Jahan, we get so busy with the details of the project that we forget the one the project honors.

From the very beginning, our world has been hesitant to receive Jesus Christ with open hearts and open arms. One of the most crucial difficulties Jesus Christ faced from the very beginning was closed-mindedness. The thing that kept him at arm's length, that closed to him the hearts he longed to enter and sent him at last to the cross was something so simple that at first glance it does not seem like a scarlet, tragic evil . . . and yet it haunted him all the days of his life on earth—Inhospitality. No room!

Let's be honest, now. Isn't this *our* problem, yours and mine? We get so busy, so tired, so preoccupied with the incessant demands on our crowded lives that we shut out the very birth of the Master we so long to know.

Some years ago, I ran across a poem that compared and likened us and our busy lives to the little inn of Bethlehem that first Christmas night. The poet said that like that ancient Bethlehem inn, our lives are crowded to the brim. We are "full up," with no vacancies. We are so busy, so distracted, so pushed and pulled, and so preoccupied that we just do not have room for anything else. We cannot take on anything more. We are so busy "doing Christmas" that we turn away and leave out the very one Christmas is really all about. The poet then ends his poem with these words: "We have no hostile feelings [toward the King] / we merely crowd him out."

Won't you let him in this Christmas? Won't you offer him your warmest hospitality? Won't you welcome him into your life this year with open arms? Won't you receive him into your life as never before? Won't you "make room" for him?

Let me bring this closer to home for us. Let me break this down a bit and be more specific. See if you can find yourself, or someone you know, somewhere between the lines.

First, Won't You Let Him In to Your Heart?

Won't you let your heart become a manger where the Christ Child can be born afresh in you?

There is an old story about a little boy who was asked why he was a Christian. He answered, "I don't know for sure, but I think it runs in our family!"

That is a cute story, isn't it? But we need to add a footnote, and the footnote is this: We can ride on the coattails of our Christian family for just so long; and then each one of us, individually, has to make his or her own personal decision for Jesus Christ. The family can help us—and it is great when they do—but each of us, at some point, has to make that personal decision to receive Christ into our heart. It Is terrific when Granddad is a devoted Christian. It Is wonderful when Mom is a committed disciple. It Is fantastic when Dad is a consecrated churchman. But somewhere along the way, we have to make our own decision. I have to make my own decision, my own commitment, my own acceptance of Christ as my personal Savior and Lord.

Have you made that decision yet? Have you invited him into your life? Have you made room in your heart for Christ? Won't you let him come in?

It is amazing to see how many people today chase after happiness and fulfillment and spend so much time, effort, energy, and money looking in all the wrong places. One *right* place to look is in Luke 2, where we find these incredible words: "Do not be afraid; for see—I am bringing you good news of great joy for all the people: to you is born this day in the city of David, a Savior, who is the Messiah, the Lord" (2:10-11).

The powerful Roman emperor Charlemagne made an unusual request with regard to his burial. He asked to be buried sitting upright on his throne, with his crown on his head, his scepter in his hand, his royal cape draped around his shoulders, and an open book placed on his lap.

That was in A.D. 814. Nearly 200 years later, Emperor Othello wanted to see if Charlemagne's burial request had indeed been carried out. Othello ordered that the tomb be opened. They found the body just as Charlemagne had requested. At that time, however, nearly two centuries later, the crown was tilted on the skeletal head. The scepter was tarnished. The mantle was deteriorated. The body was disfigured.

Yet there, open on his lap, was the book Charlemagne had requested: the Bible! And one bony finger pointed to Matthew 16:26: "What does it profit to gain the whole world and lose your own soul?" (NKJV, paraphrased).

That is the first thought: Won't you let him in to your heart?

Second, Won't You Let Him In to Your Attitudes?

The real key in whatever we do is our *attitude*. It is really not so much *what* we do but *how* we do it, and *why*. Attitudes, motivations—that is what Jesus talked about most, and that is what he was interested in.

For example, think about the innkeeper. If, on the one hand, he had said to Mary and Joseph, "Get out of here! I'm full up and don't want to be bothered with the likes of you," that was one thing.

On the other hand, if he had said to Mary and Joseph, "Look, my friends, all my rooms here in the hotel are taken; but I see that you need help. I know a place, a quiet, private place," *that* was a different story; and the difference was in the attitude.

Attitude: It is the key to life. Change our attitudes, and we change our life. It is not just what we do but how we do it, and why. The attitude with which we do it—*that* is what counts!

One of the most beloved legends of Christmas is that of "The Little Drummer Boy." When the Christ Child was born, many beautiful gifts were brought to the manger, gifts of great beauty and splendor. But one small boy was very poor, and he had nothing to offer the Lord. This made him quite sad.

But then, he thought, *I know what I can do. I can play my drum for him!* And so he did. "Pa rum pum pum pum, pa rum pum pum pum." He played with all the love in his heart. According to the legend, as he played, the Christ Child smiled, showing that at Christmas the gift of love is the best gift of all.

You see, it was not so much *what* the drummer boy did but *how* and *why* he did it. The real key was not his drum playing— I am sure there were better drummers—it was his attitude. That attitude of love, *that* is what made the Christ Child smile.

And it still does. Won't you let him in to your heart today? And, won't you let him in to your attitudes?

Third, Won't You Let Him In to Your Relationships?

Christmas is a dramatic reminder of something the Bible says to us over and over, on page after page: Christianity is a *relational* faith.

Vertical and horizontal: We are related lovingly to God, and we are related lovingly to other people. When we become Christians, we become instruments through which God loves and reaches out to others.

God is our Father, and all people are our brothers and sisters. That is why Christmas calls so powerfully for peace on earth and love and goodwill to others. This is God's world, and we are God's family.

A pastor friend of mine recently pointed this out by showing how many times the Bible uses the little phrase "one another." In Scripture, there are at least thirty "one anothers" that characterize our life as the people of God.

When we look over the list, it becomes abundantly clear that God intends that his church be built with a strong relational emphasis. Take a look at some of these biblical "one anothers":

Love one another.
Forgive one another.
Be devoted to one another.
Forbear with one another.
Encourage one another.
Build up one another.
Don't judge one another.
Accept one another.
Counsel one another.
Pray for one another.
Care for one another.
Serve one another.
Rejoice with one another.
Weep with one another.

And on and on it goes. Over and over, the Bible reminds us of the tremendous importance of loving relationships; and the

Scriptures, without question, equate the ability to love with spiritual maturity.

Over the years, I have been something of a "people watcher"; and I have noticed that, broadly speaking, there are two kinds of people: those who are spiritually troubled and those who are spiritually healthy. Those who are spiritually troubled go through life screaming, "For God's sake, love me!" In a thousand different ways the spiritually troubled person tries desperately to get someone to love him or her. On the other hand, the person who is spiritually healthy goes through life saying, "For God's sake, let me love you!"

If we see redemptive changes in people who have been screaming, "Love me! Love me!" we can be pretty sure that the redemptive change comes when they realize that if they turn the coin over and start reaching out in love to others, then they can get the love they have been so frantically seeking all their lives. For some people, this is a hard lesson to learn. But when they learn it, it is a beautiful thing!

Jesus taught us that a long time ago. This is precisely what happened to Zacchaeus (Luke 19:1-10) and to Bartimaeus (Mark 10:46-52) and to the prodigal son (Luke 15:11-32). Grace made them gracious.

This is the good news of Christmas: We are loved, so now we can be loving.

Won't you let him in to your heart and in to your attitudes? And won't you let Christ in to all your relationships?

Fourth and Finally, Won't You Let Him In to Your Christmas?

Strange that we have to say that—"Won't you let him in to your *Christ*mas?"—but we do.

Each year at Christmas, my mind darts back to a television program I saw in 1960. (I was a mere "child" of twenty-one at the time!) Some of you may remember the show "I've Got a Secret." Garry Moore was the host. Contestants with unusual secrets would come on the show, and a panel of celebrities would ask them questions and then try to guess their secret.

One man's story that I recall is something of a parable for the way we sometimes celebrate Christmas.

A group of people in Ohio decided to give a man a surprise birthday party. They got together and organized the party in great detail. They set up several committees to take care of the arrangements for food and entertainment and decorations and all the rest.

There was a great hustle and bustle of excitement and busyness as they made ready for the big event. Finally, the evening of the party arrived; and all was in readiness. The hall was rented. The decorations were in place, and they were terrific. The food was prepared, and it looked sumptuous. The entertainment was rehearsed and ready. The friends were all gathered and excited. The lights and sound were set to perfection.

Then suddenly, they realized something. Everything had been taken care of in splendid fashion—except one thing. They had quite simply forgotten the single most important thing. They had forgotten to invite the guest of honor, so they had the party without him. This man's secret was that he had not been invited to his own birthday party!

Won't you let him in? This year, as never before, won't you let him in to your life and in to your Christmas?

Study / Discussion Questions

1. Reflect on the Christmas story in Luke 2:8-14. What does this story mean to you personally?

2. Explain this statement in your own words: "Change your attitudes, and you change your life."

3. "Christianity is a relational faith," says the author. Describe some of the ways you celebrate Christmas that express this point.

4. The author says that spiritual maturity comes with focusing less on *being* loved and more on loving *others*. Why is this so?

5. Is your Christmas celebration one at which the guest of honor is sometimes forgotten? List ways you know to ensure that Jesus is "the reason for the season."

Prayer

O God, thank you for the many gifts you give to us, including the joy of loving and being loved by you. During this season of Advent, help us to make room in our hearts for the Christ Child, that we may pass on to others your precious gift of love. Amen.

Focus for the Week

The author asks, "Won't you let your heart become a manger where the Christ Child can be born afresh in you?" This week, reflect on ways you can do just that. Pray, asking God to fill your heart with the warmth, the love, and the peace of Christ.

NOTE

[1]From *The Applause of Heaven*, by Max Lucado (Copyright © 1990 by Max Lucado); pages 131–32.

Second Week of Advent

Won't You Let Him In to Your Celebration?

Scripture: Read Matthew 1:18-25.

There is an old story about a young country boy who wanted more than anything to see the circus. So when the circus came to a nearby town, the boy's father gave him some money for a ticket. The boy rushed out early the next morning to see his first circus. He was so excited, so thrilled and anxious!

But at midday the boy returned home, and he had not spent a penny. His father asked, "What happened? Didn't you go to the circus?" "Oh, yes sir," said the boy. "The circus came right down the main street, and I got to see it all; and it didn't cost me a thing. Nobody ever took my money." The father threw up his hands and exclaimed, "Oh, no! You didn't see the circus at all! You just saw the parade! You only got a glimpse of it! You missed the main event!"

The same thing can happen to us at Christmas. We can miss the main event. We can miss the celebration. This is why the Scriptures are so important to us. The Bible reminds us of what it is all about. The Bible, when studied seriously, lifts us above the crowd, beyond the parade, and takes us to the main event, the Christ event—the depth, the graciousness, and the wonder of God's seeking love.

In his version of the Christmas story, the writer of Matthew does a very wise thing. He reaches back into the Old Testament, pulls out an old word, dusts it off, and uses it to describe the

21

Christ Child. The word is *Emmanuel*. In Matthew 1, the text reads this way: " 'They shall name him Emmanuel,' which means, 'God is with us' " (1:23).

That is the message of the Bible. That is the message of Christmas. God is with us. God seeks us out. God comes in the Christ Child to visit and redeem his people.

Do not miss it this year. Do not leave it too soon. Do not just mingle with the crowd around the edges. Do not get so caught up in the parade that you miss the main event. Pay the price, and get into the arena.

Now, the Bible and Bethlehem help us here. They describe the main event. They remind us of what it is all about. Let me encapsulate that for us with three thoughts.

At Christmas, God Comes to Us With a Word of Grace.

The word *grace* means unconditional love, love with no strings attached, love that is not earned, love freely given even when it is not deserved. In a beautiful way, Christmas shows us God's amazing grace. William Barclay put it like this:

> Jesus is the one person who can tell us what God is like. . . . Before Jesus came [people] had only vague and shadowy, and often quite wrong, ideas about God; they could only at best guess and grope; but Jesus could say, "He who has seen me has seen the Father" (John 14:9). In Jesus, we see the love, the compassion, the mercy, the seeking heart, the purity of God as nowhere else in all this world. With the coming of Jesus [at Christmas] the time of guessing is gone, and the time of certainty is come. . . . Jesus came to tell us the truth about God.[1]

This, you see, is the "good news" of Christmas. Jesus shows us what God is like, and the word is *love*. The word is *grace*. God is not an angry judge who must be appeased. He is not a power monger demanding his "pound of flesh." Rather, God is a loving father, a father who cares, a father who understands, a faithful father intensely concerned about the welfare of his

22

children. Christmas shows us in a dramatic way that God is not a harsh tyrant watching us grudgingly; he is a genuine friend watching over us graciously.

Have you ever seen the movie *Home Alone?* Only a little more than a decade old, it has become something of a Christmas classic. It is about a family living in the suburbs of Chicago who decide to go to Paris for Christmas. On the night before their scheduled departure, their electricity goes out. Consequently, their alarm clocks do not go off on time. As a result, they oversleep and are thrown late. They have to make a frenzied, mad dash to the airport.

They make their plane; but hours later, somewhere in mid-flight over the Atlantic, they realize that in their hectic rush to the airport, they took care of every detail except for one. They accidentally left their eight-year-old son and sibling, Kevin, at home alone.

Kevin survives amazingly well, and along the way he learns some important lessons about Christmas and about life. The dimension of the movie that intrigued me most of all, however, was Kevin's changing relationship with the older man who lived next door.

There were numerous scary stories about this neighbor. All the kids in the neighborhood were terrified of him. Kevin and the other children went to great lengths to steer clear of this hostile-looking man.

After being home alone for a few days, Kevin becomes quite lonely one night; so he goes to church. It is a week night. The members of the choir are rehearsing the Christmas music. Eight-year-old Kevin sits there alone, listening, his feet dangling from the pew. Suddenly, he looks to his right; and of all things—horror of horrors—seated there is that man, the scary next-door neighbor! The man sees Kevin. He recognizes him. He comes over and sits down beside Kevin. They talk. They visit. Kevin sees the man differently now. He likes him. Later, the man rescues Kevin from a dangerous situation.

Now, this is a powerful parable for Christmas. Before Jesus came, people were afraid of God. God seemed remote, harsh, vengeful. But then at Christmas, God came in Christ to befriend us. At Christmas, God came in Christ to reveal his loving spirit. At Christmas, God comes to us even now with a word of grace.

At Christmas, God Comes to Us With a Word of Judgment.

Christmas reminds us how much we need a Savior. This world is not enough. Apart from God, we are incomplete. We have sinned. We cannot make it by ourselves. We need help. We need a Savior.

A minister friend of mine had been teaching the confirmation class in his church about the different parts of a worship service. At the conclusion of the session, he gave the class members a test. He asked them, "What is the first part of the worship service?" One little boy answered, "The first part of the worship service is the adoration of sin."

This is the problem of humanity in a single phrase, isn't it, "the adoration of sin"! This is why Christ had to come, because we adored sin rather than God.

Let's be honest now. Let's go ahead and admit it. Many folks today are biblically illiterate. The Bible is a best-seller, and yet the truth is that people buy it and then do not read it. That is a judgment on us.

A professor once said, "Ignorance regarding the Bible on the part of otherwise intelligent people is one of the astounding things today." In a certain high school English class, eighty-five percent of the students could not name the four Gospels. One student said, "I only know three of them: Christianity, Hinduism, and Confusion!" At the University of Denver, a student was asked on a test to tell what he knew about Moses. He answered frankly: "All I know about Moses is that he is dead!" Our lack of knowledge of the Bible is a judgment upon us.

Worse than that, however, a more severe judgment upon us is that we have turned our backs on God. We say we love God, but we in the twenty-first-century world often seem to feel more comfortable with the so-called gods of Greek mythology. Often we spend more time with them. For example,

24

1. There is Narcissus, the mythical Greek god of self-love and self-beauty. Think of Narcissus. Then think of the millions and millions of dollars spent in our society today on the cultivation of self-beautification.

2. There is Aphrodite, the mythical Greek goddess of sensual pleasure. Think of Aphrodite. Then think of the so-called new morality and the prevalent idea these days that "anything goes that gives me pleasure," the sinfully distorted notion that people are pawns to be used and exploited for our own pleasure.

3. There is Dionysus, the mythical Greek god of wine. Think of Dionysus. Then think of the widespread, blatant, and dangerous use of alcohol, crack cocaine, marijuana, and other drugs in our modern world.

4. There is Ares, the mythical Greek god of power and war. Think of Ares. Then think of our exaltation of power; our drive for success at any price; our worship of money; and the wars, battles, and skirmishes that blacken the face of the earth.

God comes at Christmas seeking us out to show us his gracious, forgiving love and at the same time reminds us how much we need a Savior. He comes to us with a word of grace, and he also comes to us with a word of judgment.

At Christmas, God Comes to Us With a Word of Salvation.

Yes, we are sinners. Yes, we need help. Yes, we need a Savior. And yes, a Savior is given!

Do you remember Hosea? Hosea was a prophet of Israel in the eighth century B.C. Hosea knew that God was a God of justice, but he also knew that was not the end of the story. Through a heartbreaking personal experience, Hosea learned something special about God. He learned the miracle of God's redemptive love, God's saving touch.

Here is what happened. Hosea married a woman named Gomer. But Gomer was unfaithful. She gave herself to other men. She broke Hosea's heart. Then Hosea made an astonishing discovery. He realized that even though his wife had

25

betrayed him, even though she had been unfaithful to him, even though she had hurt him deeply, amazingly, he still loved her. So he went out after her; he brought her back home.

Then Hosea made a second astonishing discovery. He realized that *God's* love is like that. It has a saving, redeeming touch. Although we are unfaithful to God, although we chase after false gods, although we fall short, God still loves us. God comes and pays the price and forgives and brings us back home with a new covenant. At Christmas, God reaches out to us with a saving touch. There is a word of grace here, a word of judgment, and a word of salvation.

Now, let me conclude with this. One of the most significant breakthroughs in medical history occurred in 1967 when a South African physician, Dr. Christian Barnard, performed the first successful human heart transplant. In telling about his experiences with the earliest heart transplants, Dr. Barnard said that one of the first post-surgery requests of a recipient patient often was to see the old heart. Dr. Barnard would comply with the request, putting the heart in a jar for the patient to see. Often the patient would say, "Thank you, doctor, for taking away my old, diseased heart and giving me a new one."

Now, that is what Christmas is about. That is the main event of this sacred and holy season. God comes into the world in Jesus Christ to take away our old, diseased heart and give us a new one. That is why we call him the Great Physician.

Study / Discussion Questions

1. Describe a time when you missed "the main event" while focused on something else. What were the results? What is the main event of Christmas?

2. Give an example, from your own life or from the life of someone you know, of *grace*—unconditional love, love with no strings attached, love that is not earned, love freely given even when it is not deserved. How is the grace of God evident?

3. What examples does the author provide that suggest we bring judgment upon ourselves? In what ways does Christmas remind us that we need a Savior?

4. The author quotes William Barclay, suggesting that in the life and person of Jesus, we are able to see what God is like. What does this mean to you?

5. *Emmanuel* means "God is with us" (Matthew 1:23). The author says that this is the main message of Christmas—"God seeks us out." How do you feel God seeking you out in your life?

Prayer

Dear God, this world is not enough. Without you, we are not complete. Thank you for seeking us out by sending to us your gift of grace in the birth of your only Son, Jesus, the Savior. Help us to celebrate the main event of this Advent and Christmas season by sharing your unconditional love with others. Amen.

Focus for the Week

This week, meditate on "stepping outside" the busyness and the distractions that so often are present at this time of the year. Look for ways to make this Christmas a true celebration of "the main event," the birth of the Savior, Jesus Christ, *Emmanuel*— "God with us." Use your Bible to look for examples of God's reassurances to us that God is, and always will be, with us.

NOTE

[1] From *The Gospel of Matthew,* Volume 1, by William Barclay (The Westminster Press, 1975); page 21.

Won't You Let Him In to Your Gift-giving?

Scripture: Read Matthew 2:7-12.

One of the most charming stories I have ever read was written by a father [Rex Knowles, in *Guideposts*, December 1961; pages 12–13] whose wife went Christmas shopping one afternoon and left Dad at home with the children. The father was enjoying the quiet time at home, reclining on the couch in the den, half-dozing and half-watching a college football game. Suddenly, the children disturbed his peace by loudly announcing, "Daddy, we have a play to put on. Do you want to see it?"

"Daddy didn't, but he knew that he would have to; so he went into the living-room and sat down, a one-man audience." He saw quickly that it was a Christmas play. At the foot of the piano bench was a flashlight. It was turned on, and wrapped in "swaddling clothes" and lying in a shoe box.

Then six-year-old "Rex came in wearing Daddy's bathrobe and carrying a mop-handle." He was followed by ten-year-old Nancy, who announced, "I'm Mary, and this is Joseph." Then four-year-old "Trudy entered with pillow-cases over her arms which she waved about, saying, 'I am an angel.'"

Finally, in came eight-year-old Anne, riding a camel. "At least, she moved as though she was riding a camel, because she had on her mother's high-heeled shoes. She was bedecked in all the jewelry available and carried a pillow," on which were three Christmas presents.

She went over and bowed before the "Holy Family" and announced, "I am all three Wise Men. I bring precious gifts: gold, circumstance and mud!"

"That was all. The play was over. But Daddy did not laugh." He did not correct his daughter. Rather, he prayed because he realized "how near his little daughter had come to the truth" of Christmas. Of course she had meant to say, "I bring precious gifts of gold, frankincense, and myrrh"; but even as she mixed up the words, she had gotten right to the heart of Christmas.[1]

She had underscored the message of Christmas because Christmas reminds us that we can indeed bring to God our gold; our circumstances; and, yes, even our mud!

Let me show you what I mean.

First, Christmas Reminds Us That We Can Bring to God Our Gold.

Over the years, gold has come to symbolize our very best possessions, our substance, our material value. From the time the wise men brought their gifts to the manger, Christmas has been a time of giving—giving gifts to one another, gifts to those we love, gifts to the needy, gifts to those less fortunate, gifts to neighbors, gifts to coworkers, gifts to aunts and uncles and cousins and nephews and nieces, and even gifts to pets.

Santa is not the only one who is "making a list and checking it twice." We all are poring over our gift lists, giving much time, effort, and energy to selecting just the right gifts to give to those we love. And that is fine; I love that, and I am all for it!

But do we sometimes forget what it is really all about? Do we sometimes leave out the single most important thing? Do we sometimes fail to include the one whose birthday we are celebrating? Do we sometimes leave Christ and his church off our Christmas gift list?

A few years ago, I ran across a beautiful story about this that makes the point so well. The story was called "Where's His?" and it goes something like this.

One Christmas Eve, a woman of modest but comfortable means was showing a young girl, a visitor to the woman's home, her Christmas decorations. The girl asked, "What's Christmas?" The woman explained to her that Christmas is Christ's birthday; and she showed the girl her Christmas tree, complete with the family's Christmas presents underneath. In one beautiful box was a hunting jacket for the woman's husband. In another attractive package was a game for her granddaughter. In another lovely box, there was a gift for the woman's son. And in yet another, there was something for a niece.

One by one, the woman named off each present, cheerfully explaining to the little girl what each gift was and for whom it was intended. When she had finished, the little girl was silent for a moment as she thought over the pile of presents. Then, quietly, she asked, "Where's his?"

"What do you mean?" asked the woman. "Have I forgotten someone? I've gone over that list so many times. Who have I forgotten?" The little girl replied, "Didn't you say Christmas is Christ's birthday? Where is his present?"

You see, Christmas reminds us that we, like the wise man, can bring to the Christ Child and his church our gold. We can put him and his church on our gift list.

Second, Christmas Reminds Us That We Can Bring to God Our Circumstances.

That is, we can bring to God our joys and our sorrows, our victories and our defeats, our biggest concerns and our smallest worries.

A couple of years ago, while on a speaking engagement in another city, I had breakfast with an old college classmate named Jimmy. He had heard that I was in town, and he took me to breakfast. I learned that he is now a sales representative for a large national company.

During our visit, Jimmy told me about a recent experience he had had with his new sales manager. He was driving his new boss around town when they happened to pass near Jimmy's home. Jimmy asked the new sales manager if he would like to stop by his house and meet his family. "My wife is baking an apple pie," Jimmy said; "and the children will just be coming in from school. Would you like to drop in?"

Jimmy was stunned by the new sales manager's irate and hostile reply. He said, "Let's get one thing straight right now: I'm not interested in your home or your family. I'm not interested in your wife or your children. I'm not interested in you personally at all or in any of the circumstances of your life. All I'm interested in is results. All I'm interested in about you is your sales record!"

Jimmy said, "That really hurt. I felt like someone had slapped me across the face. But you know, I realized something. I realized that God is the opposite of that! God is interested in my home and my family. God is interested in my wife and my children. God does care about me personally. He is interested in all of the circumstances of my life."

Jimmy was right. That is the "good news" of Christmas. God cares, and God is with us. The word of Christmas is *Emmanuel*—"God with us." God is with us in every circumstance of life—and indeed, even *beyond* this life. Nothing, not even death, can separate us from God and his love.

We can bring our gold to the manger. But we can also bring our joys and our sorrows to the Christ Child.

We can give God our gold. And we can also give him our circumstances.

Third and Finally, Christmas Reminds Us That We Can Bring to God Not Only Our Gold and Our Circumstances But, Yes, We Can Even Bring to God Our Mud!

That is, we can bring to God our weaknesses, our failures, our foibles, our mistakes, our inadequacies, our sins. We can even bring to the manger our "mud," "our clay feet"; and somehow God, through the miracle of his grace, can redeem them and reshape them.

Some time ago, I was working late in my office. Everyone else had gone home for the day. I was at my desk when I felt someone looking at me. Have you ever had that experience? I just felt the presence of another person. Looking up, I saw standing in the doorway a young woman who appeared to be in her early twenties. She was crying softly. She said, "You don't know me, and I'm not a member of this church; but I need desperately to tell someone my story. Let me tell you what a terrible thing I've done, and then I want to ask you one question."

Through tears, her story unfolded. She had married at eighteen. The marriage had lasted two years. Her husband had deserted her. Hurt, scared, and confused, for a time she had wallowed in self-pity. But then she had become so lonely and so disoriented that she had taken up a lifestyle that was totally the opposite of every moral value she had ever been taught, a lifestyle so sordid that she could not even look at me as she described it.

Earlier that evening as she was driving through the streets of the city, she had seen the steeple of our church; and suddenly she was jolted by the reality of what her life had become. It hit her; it all caved in on her. As she thought back over the last few weeks and what she had been doing, she was ashamed, sorry, penitent.

She pulled into our church parking lot at that very moment and came to my office and told me her story. She was obviously penitent. Then came the question: "How could God ever forgive me for what I've done?" she asked.

I replied, "God already forgives you. The question is, Can you forgive yourself? Can you, in faith, accept God's forgiveness? Can you learn from this? Can you make a new start with your life?"

She still seemed unsure of God's forgiveness; so I said, "Let me ask you to do something. I want you to imagine that you are my daughter and that you have just told me your story, exactly as you told it before. As a father, I would have two choices: (1) I could say, 'Get out of my sight! You have dishonored our family! I disown you! Get out!'; or (2) I could reach out to you with compassion and say, 'Oh, I am so sorry this has happened. I love you, and I want to help you! Let me help you make a new beginning with your life!' "

33

Then I asked her, "Now, which one of those do you think I would do?"

She replied, "I think you would do the second."

"Why do you think that?" I asked her.

"Because," she said, "even though I don't know you too well, I do know that you are a father and that you love your children."

"Precisely!" I said to her. "And if *I* am capable of that kind of love and forgiveness, how much more is God!"

That is what Christmas is about. Christ comes to show us that God is a loving Father, not a vindictive judge who must be appeased. God is a gracious, merciful, loving Father to whom, in faith, we can bring our gold, our circumstances, and even our mud. God can take those gifts and redeem them and reshape them and use them for good. That is the good news of Christmas!

Study / Discussion Questions

1. Describe a time when you experienced true joy in gift-giving. What gift did you give? How was the gift received?

2. The author encourages us to draw closer to God and to open ourselves up to God in a number of ways. For what reasons, do you believe, do we so often fail or neglect to do this in our lives?

3. Make a list of the gifts you need to bring to God—your "gold" (material possessions), your "circumstances" (joys and sorrows, biggest concerns and smallest worries), and your "mud" (weaknesses, failures, mistakes, sins). [**Note:** Share your list with someone only if you feel comfortable doing so.] What could be the results of your turning these things over to God?

4. In the author's story, how did the young woman's view of God begin to change? In what ways do you believe God can take the negative or burdensome things you bring and reshape them to be used for good?

Prayer

O God, just as you were a loving Father to your Son, Jesus Christ, you are also a loving Parent to us. Thank you for always being there, during Advent and throughout the year, to welcome and embrace us. Give us courage and strength to give our lives completely to you; and grant us peace in knowing that when we give you the "gifts" of our burdens, we will not have to worry about them anymore. Amen.

Focus for the Week

This week, focus on the things in your life that you need to give to God. (You may begin with the list you created in question number 3 on page 34, adding to it as you go; or you may start from scratch.) Pray for God's direction, that God will take the things over which you are releasing control and use them for good.

NOTE

[1] Adapted from *God's Time and Ours,* by Leonard Griffith (Abingdon Press, 1964); page 68.

Won't You Let Him In to Your Christmas?

Scripture: Read Luke 2:8-14.

In the golden days of the settling of the west, an old prospector was exploring new territory looking for gold. As he pulled his mule along behind him, he trudged over a rise and suddenly came to an abrupt halt at the very edge of the Grand Canyon. He could not believe his eyes; he gawked at the sight before him!

He had never in his life seen anything like this: the vast chasm, a mile deep, eighteen miles across, and more than two hundred miles long—so awesome, so incredible, so colossal, so amazing, it took his breath away. He looked at the grandeur of the Grand Canyon in reverent silence for a brief moment and then he turned to his mule and said, "Thunderation! Something big's done happened here!'

That is the way I feel when I look at Christmas: the sights, the sounds, the symbols, the fragrances, the traditions, the lights, the decorations, the parades, the parties, the plays, the pageants, the music, the worship services—all celebrating the birth of a little baby in a little town called Bethlehem some two thousand years ago.

When you really see all of that coming together and stretching all around the globe and touching the lives of millions and millions of people on every continent, it makes you want to shout with that old prospector, "Thunderation! Something big's done happened here!"

A man and a woman were standing on the corner of 5th Avenue and 57th Street in New York City. It was Christmastime, and the Christmas rush was going on in full force before their very eyes. They were waiting for the traffic light to change. The man was obviously irritated by the crowds and the hubbub and the trafffic. In frustration, he growled, "This town is totally disorganized. Look at this traffic! It's terrible! Awful! Something ought to be done about it. It's just ridiculous!!"

The woman, on the other hand, had a different view altogether. She responded to his outburst by saying, "You know, when you really stop to think about it, it's not ridiculous at all. It's astonishing! It's amazing! The romance of it is extraordinary! There was a baby born in a peasant family in a little out-of-the-way village halfway around the world from here. The parents had no money, no clout, no prestige, no social standing, yet, two thousand years later, their little baby creates a traffic jam on 5th Avenue, one of the most sophisticated streets in the world. This irritates you? It should fascinate you! It should amaze you!" Do you know what that woman in New Yok was saying? She was saying, "Thunderation! Something big's done happened here!"

In essence, that is what the shepherds were thinking and saying to one another on that silent and holy night so long ago. They saw the angel on that first Christmas night. They heard the Savior was being born in near-by Bethlehem. They heard the music from heaven, praising God for this gracious gift of his Son.

And then the shepherds said, "Let us go now to Bethlehem and see this thing that has taken place, which the Lord has made known to us" (Luke 2:15). They rushed over there and found Mary and Joseph and the baby lying in a manger; and when they saw it, they knew for sure that something big had happened here.

Well, what is this big thing that has happened? Incredibly, this: The God who made the universe, the One who set the moon and stars in place, the One who breathed into us the breath of life came to earth in the form of a little baby to visit and redeem his people.

Remember how John put it: "For God so loved the world that he gave his only Son, so that everyone who believes in him may not perish but may have eternal life" (3:16). Talk about a Christmas present! Talk about a gift that keeps on giving! Talk about a gift of love! This is the best Christmas present of all.

Then remember how Luke expressed it in his Christmas story:

> And in that region there were shepherds out in the field, keeping watch over their flock by night. And an angel of the Lord appeared to them, and the glory of the Lord shone around them, and they were filled with fear. And the angel said to them, "Be not afraid; for behold, I bring you good news of a great joy which will come to all the people; for to you is born this day in the city of David a Savior, who is Christ the Lord. And this will be a sign for you: you will find a babe wrapped in swaddling cloths and lying in a manger." And suddenly there was with the angel a multitude of the heavenly host praising God and saying, "Glory to God in the highest, / and on earth peace [and good will to all]." (2:8-14, adapted).

The story tells us that the Christ Child was "wrapped in swaddling cloths and lying in a manger"; but we know something deeper, don't we? Before that, this first and best Christmas present was wrapped in heaven.

This is God's Christmas gift for each one of us. In the obscure form of a tiny baby born in a stable, the Author of all life is saying, "Here—straight from heaven—this is the best I have. Take this gift, receive this, embrace this. I give this gift to you because I love you so much."

This sacrificial gift from God is offered graciously and lovingly, but let me hurry to say that *we* have to do *our* part. We have to accept it. We have to receive it. We have to treasure it. God will not force it on us. We have to reach out in faith and embrace and cherish and celebrate and receive into our hearts this amazing gift.

One of the greatest artists of all time was Pablo Picasso. After he became established as one of the world's great artists, every work that Picasso created was worth a fortune.

One day, he walked into a carpenter's shop to order a new wardrobe for his home. He explained to the carpenter that he wanted a mahogany wardrobe that would fit into the corner of his bedroom.

The carpenter listened carefully but appeared confused. Picasso again described precisely what he wanted and how he wanted the wardrobe to look, but again the carpenter looked confused and unsure. Picasso tried to describe it a third time, with the same results. The carpenter did not seem to understand.

Finally, Pablo Picasso grabbed a pencil and a piece of scratch paper and sketched out precisely what he wanted and how he wanted the wardrobe to look in his bedroom. "Oh yes, *now* I understand," said the carpenter.

"Well, how much do I owe you?" Picasso asked.

"Nothing at all," the carpenter said. "Just sign the sketch!"

The carpenter was a smart man. He knew that the best gift of all is that gift in which we give a part of ourselves. That is what God taught us at the first Christmas. When we give to others a portion of ourselves, that is a gift wrapped in heaven.

By being more specific, let me show you what I mean.

There Is the Gift of Acceptance.

A number of years ago, here in Houston, the Bear Bryant Coach of the Year Award was presented to a young Terry Bowden, the first-year head football coach at Auburn University. Terry Bowden had taken a struggling program that was on probation and led his team to a season in which the team was undefeated.

Interestingly, Terry Bowden's father, Bobby Bowden, who is the head football coach at Florida State University, was also nominated for the award. There was a lot of good-natured joking and teasing at the banquet about this father and son being considered for the same prestigious award. And, of course, when the son, Terry, won, nobody in the room was happier or prouder than his dad.

In his acceptance speech, Terry Bowden thanked his team, his fellow coaches, Auburn University, and then his family.

"I owe so much to my parents," he said. "Many of you in this room know my mother, and you know how special she is; but let me tell you about my father." He said, "My parents always took us five kids to church. Even when we were on a trip, they took us to church. Once while on vacation, we went to this church that was a little more emotional than we were used to. The minister was shouting and pounding the pulpit, and he began to look around the congregation for someone to single out; and he spotted my father.

"Mom and Dad had marched us down to the front pew. Mom was on one end, Dad on the other end, with the five kids squeezed in between to be sure we would behave in church. The preacher pointed dramatically to my dad, and this conversation took place.

"You there—Do you have faith?" "Yes, I have faith," Dad answered. The preacher said, "If I put a two-by-four board down there on the floor, do you have enough faith to walk across it?" "Yes, I could do that."

"But," said the preacher, "What if I took that same two-by-four board and placed it across the top of the two tallest buildings in New York City, would you have enough faith to walk across it then?" "No, I don't have that much faith," Dad answered.

"But, what if somebody were standing on the other end," said the preacher, "and were dangling one of your children off the side. Would you cross the board then?"

Terry Bowden said that his father turned and looked down the pew at his five kids and said, "Which one?"

Now, of course, Terry Bowden was just kidding around; the Bowdens are a very close-knit, loving family. But the point I want to make is this: Our Father God does not ask, "Which one?" God does not ask, "Which one should I lay my life on the line for?" God so loved the world; he wants to bring us all into the circle.

God comes with the open arms of acceptance for all of us. To each one of us, God says, "You are valued. You are included. You are wanted. You are precious to me."

We have to do our part, however. We have to accept God's acceptance of us. We have to receive this gracious gift. We have to welcome God into our hearts and lives with faith. This Christmas present is offered to us from God. When we receive it and live in that spirit and pass that gift on to others, we are giving them a Christmas present wrapped in heaven: the gift of acceptance.

If you want to give something special to someone at Christmas this year—to your children, your parents, your neighbors, your coworkers, your friends—just say to them, "You are valued. You are included. You are wanted and needed. You are precious to me."

However you want to say it, just express that; and you will give them a Christmas present wrapped in heaven: the gift of acceptance.

There Is the Gift of Forgiveness.

Steven Spielberg's movie *Schindler's List* is a graphic, shocking, unflinching depiction of the twentieth century's most staggering horror: the methodical, brutal extermination of millions of human beings in the Nazi death camps of World War II. Oskar Schindler was a most unlikely hero; but through the efforts of this one man, some 1,200 persons were saved from certain death. He put them to work in his factory where he could protect them.

One of the most powerful moments in the movie is when Oskar Schindler is in conversation with the commander of the labor camp in Krakow, Poland. They are talking about power; and the commander, in his swaggering way, brags about the authority he has over the people under his control. Then a man comes before him. The commander has the absolute authority to kill that man, exterminate that man, if he so chooses. And the commander has been in the habit of doing just that—brutally killing people right and left, with no conscience at all.

But Oskar Schindler says to him, in not so many words, "Oh no, Commander, you are wrong. That is not power. *Anyone* could do that. But to have a man come before you and to say,

'I could take your life if I so choose, but, no, instead, I pardon you!' *That,* Commander, is power!"

It is indeed the power of forgiveness, and that is the Christmas gift God offers us.

It is said that Martin Luther once became so frustrated with the evil he saw going on around him that he shouted, "If I were God and the world had treated me as it treated Him, I would kick the wretched thing to pieces!" *Luther* might have responded this way to the world, but not *God.* God comes into the world offering the gift of forgiveness. "I pardon you. I forgive you. I want to reclaim you."

That is the gift God offers, but we have to do our part. We have to accept the gift in faith. When we accept forgiveness and offer forgiveness to others and live in the spirit of forgiveness, we are doing a Godlike thing. We are offering a "Christmas present wrapped in heaven"—the gift of forgiveness.

There is the gift of acceptance, and there is the gift of forgiveness.

There Is the Gift of Love.

Love came down at Christmas. Robert Smith of Stroudsburg, Pennsylvania, tells a true story that says it all. Listen closely to his words. (Thanks to Don Shelby, December 24, 1992 sermon, "The Power of Love.")

It's been thirty years since I last saw her, but in memory she's still there every holiday season. I especially feel her presence when I receive my first Christmas card.

I was twelve years old and Christmas was only two days away. The season's first blanket of white magnified the excitement. I dressed hurriedly, for the snow was waiting. What would I do first—build a snowman, slide down the hill or just throw flakes in the air and watch them flutter down?

Our family's station wagon pulled into the driveway and Mom called me over to help with the groceries. When we finished carrying in the bags, she said, "Bob, here are Mrs. Hildebrandt's groceries."

No other instructions were necessary. As far back as I could remember, Mom shopped for Mrs. Hildebrandt's food and I delivered it. Our ninety-five-year-old neighbor, who lived alone, was crippled from arthritis and could take only a few steps with a cane.

Even though she was old, [feeble] and didn't play baseball, I liked Mrs. Hildebrandt. I enjoyed talking with her; more accurately, I enjoyed listening to her. She told me wonderful stories about her life—about a steepled church in the woods and buggy rides on Sunday afternoons and her family farm without electricity and running water.

She always gave me a dime for bringing in her groceries. It got so that I would refuse only halfheartedly, knowing she would insist. Five minutes later I'd be across the street in Bayer's Candy Store.

As I headed over with the grocery bags, I decided this time would be different, though. I wouldn't accept any money. This would be my Christmas present to her. Impatiently, I rang the doorbell. Almost inaudible at first were the slow, weary shuffles of her feet and the slower thump of her cane. The chain on the door rattled and the door creaked open. Two shiny eyes peered from the crack.

"Hello, Mrs. Hildebrandt," I said. "It's me, Bob. I have your groceries." "Oh yes, come in, come in," she said cheerfully. "Put the bag on the table."

I did so more hurriedly than usual, because I could almost hear the snow calling me back outside. She sat at the table, picked the items out of the bag and told me where to set them on the shelves. I usually enjoyed doing this, but it was snowing.

As we continued, I began to realize how lonely she was. Her husband had died more than twenty years ago, she had no children and her only living relative was a nephew in Philadelphia who never visited her.

Nobody ever called on her at Christmas. There would be no tree, no presents. For her, Christmas was now only a date on the calendar. She offered me a cup of tea, which she did every time I brought the groceries. Well, maybe the snow could wait.

We sat and talked about what Christmas was like when she

was a child. Together, we traveled back in time and an hour passed before I knew it.

"Well, Bob, you must be wanting to play outside in the snow," she said as she reached for her purse, fumbling for the right coin. "No, Mrs. Hildebrandt, I can't take your money this time. You can use it for more important things," I resisted. She looked at me and smiled. "What more important thing could I use this money for if not to give it to a friend at Christmas?" she asked and then placed a whole quarter in my hand.

I tried to give it back, but she would have none of it. I hurried out the door and ran over to Bayer's Candy Store with my fortune. I had no idea what to buy—comic books, chocolate soda, ice cream. But then, out of the corner of my eye, I spotted something. It was a Christmas card with an old country church in the woods on the cover. It was just like the church Mrs. Hildebrandt described to me, and I knew I had to buy it.

I handed Mr. Bayer my quarter and borrowed a pen to sign my name. "For your girlfriend?" Mr. Bayer asked. I started to say "No," but quickly changed my mind. "Well, yes, I guess so."

As I walked back across the street with my gift, I was so proud of myself. I felt like I had just hit a home run to win the World Series. No, I felt a lot better than that!

I rang Mrs. Hildebrandt's doorbell. The sounds of shuffling again reached my ears—the door cracked open. "Hello, Mrs. Hildebrandt," I said as I handed her the card. "Merry Christmas to you!" Her hands trembled as she slowly opened the envelope. She studied the card and began to cry. "Thank you very much," she said in almost a whisper. "And, Merry Christmas to you!"

On a cold and windy afternoon a few weeks later, the ambulance arrived next door. My mom said they found Mrs. Hildebrandt in bed. She had died peacefully in her sleep. Her night table light was still on when they found her, and it illuminated a solitary Christmas card, a Christmas card with an old country church in the woods on the cover.

The gifts of acceptance, forgiveness, and love: These are the best Christmas presents of all, for these are the presents "wrapped in heaven."

Study / Discussion Questions

1. What does the author say was the best Christmas present God gave us? How was this a gift "wrapped in heaven"? What, according to the author, is our responsibility in relation to this amazing gift?

2. What role has the gift of acceptance played in your life? How can you share the gift of acceptance with others?

3. How is forgiveness powerful? Reflect on the people in your life you wish would forgive you and/or the people in your life whom you need to forgive. This Advent season, what steps can you take toward forgiveness?

4. How is God's love evident in the Christmas story (Luke 2:8-14)? In what ways can we show Godlike love to others, at Christmastime and beyond?

Prayer

Dear God, thank you for giving us the special gift of your Son, Jesus Christ. Thank you for the acceptance, the forgiveness, and the love Jesus brings to us. Help us to let Jesus into our hearts and our lives this season like never before, that we may share with others the amazing gifts you give and the joyous, true celebration of Christmas. Amen.

Focus for the Week

We have been given the best gift of God in the birth of Jesus Christ, *Emmanuel*. Each day, reflect on your decision to let him into your life. Pray that God will help you to show acceptance, forgiveness, and love; and work toward sharing God's gift to you by giving the best of yourself to others.